VALUES FOR SUCCESS

Stories of Kindness

Compiled by Chen Jia
Illustrated by Huang Qingrong
Translated by Geraldine Goh

ASIAPAC • SINGAPORE

Publisher
ASIAPAC BOOKS PTE LTD
996 Bendemeer Road #06-08/09
Singapore 339944
Tel: (65) 392 8455
Fax: (65) 392 6455
Email apacbks@singnet.com.sg

Visit us at our Internet home page
www.asiapacbooks.com

First published January 2000

© 2000 ASIAPAC BOOKS, SINGAPORE
ISBN 981-229-098-2

All rights reserved. No part of this publication may be reproduced, stored in a retrieval system, or transmitted, in any form or by any means, electronic, mechanical, photocopying, recording, or otherwise, without the prior written permission of the publisher. Under no circumstances shall it be rented, resold or redistributed. If this copy is defective, kindly exchange it at the above address.

Cover design by Illusion Creative Studio
Body text in 8/9 pt Helvetica
Printed in Singapore by
Chung Printing

Publisher's Note

Whilst much emphasis is placed on quick information in our knowledge-based economy, any "learning nation" must have the wisdom to discern critical attitudes which will help her people withstand the stress of modern living.

In his bestselling book *Principle-Centered Leadership*, Stephen R. Covey contends that the leader of the new millennium is one who creates a culture or a value system centred upon principles. Conceived along this line, each book in *Values for Success* series centres on one of the eight values which form an integral part of the cultural treasury of Chinese ethical ideals: **loyalty, filial piety, kindness (benevolence), love, propriety, righteousness, integrity** and **honour** (忠、孝、仁、爱、礼、义、廉、耻).

Kindness (*ren*) is human-heartedness, the essence of which is to love others. It embraces all-round virtue: humanity, magnanimity, consideration for others, conscience, righteousness and love. We therefore laud the government's efforts to promote a kind and gracious society, and sharing these aims, we are pleased to present to you this collection of stories on kindness. You will read about Chinese historical figures who were led by their human-heartedness to do kind deeds for others. We hope they will inspire you to bring about happiness to those around you by being tolerant, compassionate and kind, thus making this world a better place to live in.

We would like to express our gratitude to Huang Qingrong for his vivid and lively illustrations, Chen Jia for the compilation, Prof Chen Junmin for the introduction and Geraldine Goh for the translation. Our thanks, too, to the production team for putting in their best efforts in the publication of this book.

The Singapore Kindness Movement

The Singapore Kindness Movement (SKM) was initiated in response to our Prime Minister Goh Chok Tong's call on Singaporeans to develop into a more caring and gracious society by the new millennium. PM Goh announced the SKM pilot project in July 1996, when he launched the Singapore Courtesy Campaign. Some 2,000 students from the uniformed groups in 20 secondary schools participated in the pilot project.

The Movement was launched in January 1997 to all 80,000 plus secondary school students. The SKM was officially registered as a non-profit organisation on 31 January 1997.

Mission
The mission of the SKM is to inspire graciousness through spontaneous acts of kindness, making life more pleasant for everyone.

Objectives
- To encourage all Singaporeans to be more kind and considerate.
- To enhance public awareness of acts of kindness.
- To influence and raise the standards of social behaviour in our society.
- To promote and build membership in the movement.

The Council
The SKM is run by a council of members from the private and public sectors. It is supported by the Ministry of Information and the Arts and funded by a government grant. To date the SKM has a total membership of 362, comprising schools, corporations and individuals.

Activities
There are different programmes for educational institutions. On satisfactory completion of the programmes they receive badges and certificates to recognise their efforts and to motivate them. There are also corresponding programmes for primary schools and kindergartens. Programmes for nursery children are also being developed.

SKM also organises the annual SKM Week, and annual seminar for members and non-member schools as well as corporations. The numbers participating have been increasing. Among SKM's publications are *Talktime,* a thrice-yearly newsletter with a print run of 10,000 to 12,000 copies, *The 300 Nuggets on Kindness Sayings* and *My Kindness Diary.*

The focus of the Movement is on small acts of kindness — actions that anyone can do out of goodwill or consideration for others. A little kindness can go a long way to making life more pleasant for everyone. These little gestures make for a more gracious society. This is the message of the SKM. For more information and membership application, please check our homepage: http://www.sg/skm.

The Secretariat
1 December 1999

About the Compiler

Chen Jia 陈 嘉, a native of Chongqing, China, was born in 1957. After graduating from the University of Xinjiang in 1982, she became a lecturer in Nanjing College for Population Programme Management. Currently a Chinese teacher in a language centre in Singapore, Chen Jia has a passion for Chinese history and literature. Some of her writings have been published in *Lianhe Zaobao* 《联合早报》.

About the Illustrator

Huang Qingrong 黄 庆 荣, also known by the name Ng Keng Yeow, was born in 1975 in Malaysia. He graduated from the One Academy of Communication Design in 1996. In 1997, he worked as an assistant to Taiwanese cartoonist Ai Leidi 艾雷迪. In the same year, he won the second prize in the Fourth Newcomer Comic Award by Sharp Point Publishing. He then came to Singapore to work with Singapore cartoonist Teo Seng Hock in the *Water Margin* comic series (six volumes) published by Asiapac Books. His other works under the *Values for Success* series include *Stories of Integrity* and *Stories of Love*. Books on supreme wisdom are in the pipeline. Huang Qingrong has also produced short comics on love and science fiction which have been serialised in a Malaysian comic magazine.

Introduction

The turn of the century sees the world on the threshold of change, the most significant of which must surely be the transformation of tradition. The issue here is that fundamental cultural values have shifted.

The shift has brought the world joy as well as pain. We take pride when great advancement is made in science and technology, and when our nation grows strong and wealthy. But these achievements bring with them insatiable desire for material gains. Moral values plunge and the human spirit is lost.

In a society experiencing fast-changing modes of living, can cultural values stay intact and yet still be applicable to a modern society as well as a traditional one? Can these values still be depended on spiritually as a pillar of support?

I believe they can. If these values were unpragmatic, would the Chinese have possibly flourished from generation to generation? Western sociologists maintain that tradition ensures public order and is a signature of a rich civilisation. Tradition will never die out as even discarded values and customs will make a comeback from time to time.

Linked to a common theme — the Confucian values of benevolence and love, and benevolence and humanity — these values are lauded by the West as well as the East, and have become the prime interests of all mankind.

A big contribution of Confucianism to world civilisation is its creation of a comprehensive set of moral principles. Benevolence, regarded as the highest virtue, connotes loyalty, forgiveness, filial piety, respect, generosity, good faith, resourcefulness and kindness. Its basic meaning thus embraces a love for one's fellowmen.

From benevolence and love in relationships, three mainstays and five constant virtues — core values of Chinese moral principles — are created. The three mainstays refer to the powers of the ruler over his subjects, the father over his son, and the husband over his wife. They reflect clearly a traditional society that practises sex and class discrimination. With the dissolution of the old laws, these became obsolete and gave way to the five constant values — benevolence, righteousness, propriety, wisdom and good faith — which harmonise human relationships.

Though emphasis is made on differences in rank, position and ties, harmony to maintain good relationship is not forgotten. There is a sharing of duty and responsibility. The aim is to be fair and reasonable — not primarily to protect the interests of the principal over the subordinate but to strike a balance in the relationship. When one party destroys the bond built on moral principles, the responsibility of the other party too is shattered. Clearly, the five constant virtues have played an active role in maintaining harmonious relationships in the traditional society. This leads to the concept of the eight virtues which emerged during the Qing era: filial piety, brotherly respect, loyalty, trust, propriety, righteousness, integrity and honour.

In the early years of the Republican Age, Dr Sun Yat-sen advocated freedom, equality, fraternity and humanitarianism. On the other hand, he also stressed cooperation, loyalty, filial piety, benevolence, love, trust, righteousness, harmony and peace. Traditional moral values gain greater distinction and these virtues, built upon a new foundation, have been given new meaning and rank. They connote a caring heart, humanitarianism, high moral values and perfection of character.

In disengaging oneself from a traditional society through modernisation, the importance of such values has been in differing degrees once again affirmed. A stable society, a good clean government, racial harmony, successful careers, family happiness — these things are all closely related to one's moral cultivation and cultural standard.

To foster the best values of Asian society, Asiapac has made an attempt to reinterpret these eight virtues — loyalty, filial piety, kindness (benevolence), love, propriety, righteousness, integrity, honour — under the *Values for Success* series. It is hoped that the stories in the series will inspire readers, especially young readers, to create a life of success and happiness. It is thus with great joy that I recommend it to the readers. Thought-provoking and presented in comic form, the historical tales will give new sparkle and content to our rich and active cultural life.

Professor Chen Junmin

Contents

Shang Tang Makes Three Openings in the Net 1
商汤捕鸟网开三面

Marquis Wen Assesses Tax Collection 11
魏文候纳赋谙民情

Sun Shu'ao Opens Up Protected Land 21
孙叔敖仁爱开山泽

Prefect Gong Appeases the Bandits 33
龚太守施仁息盗

Wen Weng Educates the People 43
文翁立学教化蜀民

Chen Shi Gives Bolts of Cloth to a Thief 53
陈寔馈绢教海贼人

**Physician Dong Feng
and the Almond Trees 63**
良医董奉杏树成林

**Du Fu Lets Old Lady
Pick Dates 71**
杜甫善待扑枣老妇

**Fan Zhongyan Puts
Concern Before Enjoyment 83**
先忧后乐的范仲淹

Su Shi Paints the Fans 91
苏轼画扇急人之难

**Xu Rang's Happiness Lies
in Giving a Helping Hand 103**
仁者须让助人为乐

**Li Shizhen's *Encyclopedia
of Herbs* 109**
李时珍为民著本草

KINDNESS

The character for *ren* (仁) comprises the component 人 (human being), denoting the legs and trunk of a person, and a pair of horizontal strokes (二), denoting "two". It suggests the human-heartedness or kindness that one person shows to another. *Ren* thus embraces kindness and humanity. To be kind and humane is to be benevolent, a quality which Confucius ranks as a special kind of virtue, that is, it embraces all the virtues combined. A "man of *ren*" is thus a "man of all-round virtue". Kindness therefore encompasses a love for our fellowmen, a virtue which prompts us to do good to others, as we would like them to do to us.

Shang Tang Makes Three Openings in the Net

Shang Tang, founder of the Shang Dynasty, was a ruler of loving kindness. He cared deeply for his people and showed humanity even to animals.

Chirp! Chirp!

What's going on?

Why is there such a big net surrounding the trees?

Birds from all over, come fly into my net.

The story of Shang Tang making three openings in the net to free some of the birds quickly spread.

Impressed with Shang Tang's kind and noble character, his people showed him even greater support.

With overwhelming support from his people, Shang Tang toppled the despotic ruler of the Xia Dynasty and established the Shang Dynasty.

Marquis Wen Assesses Tax Collection

Marquis Wen of the State of Wei was a caring man who ruled during the Eastern Zhou Dynasty. Reports submitted to him by his officials often underwent his close scrutiny. He was concerned about the well-being of his people and governed his land with kindness.

My Lord, the taxes for the year have been collected. The sum collected from Xihe County is thrice last year's.

The Prime Minister

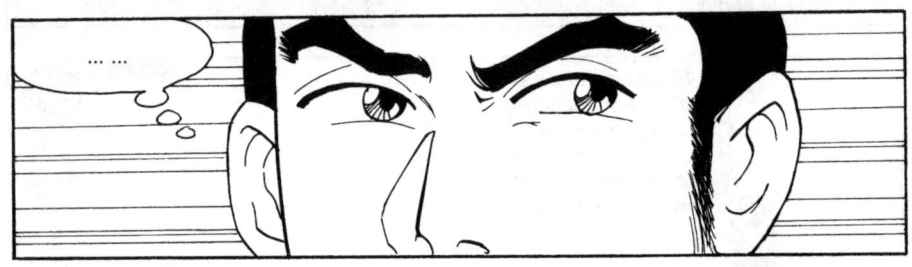

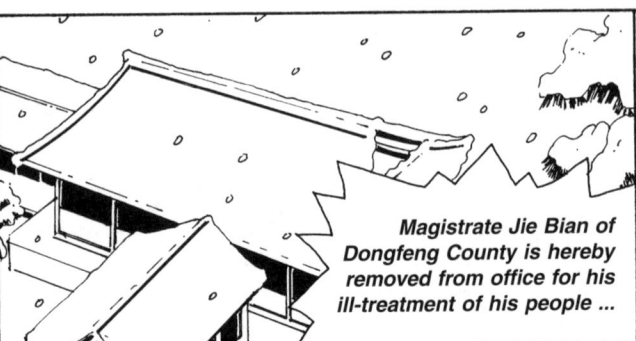

Sun Shu'ao Opens Up Protected Land

Sun Shu'ao was the Prime Minister of Chu during the Eastern Zhou Dynasty. He had a kind heart and was always mindful of others' needs. Thus he became known as the good and kind prime minister.

One day, little Sun Shu'ao was playing hide-and-seek with his friends when ...

No!

Aaargh ... A snake!

Heave!

No! I've got to kill the snake or Xiaozhu will be hurt.

Thud!

Sun Shu'ao killed the snake instantly. He dug a hole to bury it.

* Government office in feudal China.

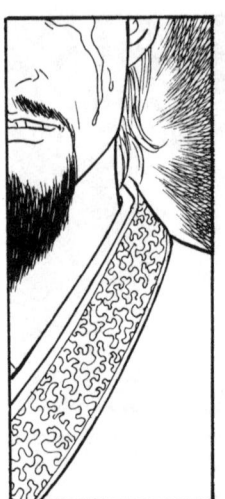

Prefect Gong Appeases the Bandits

Gong Sui was an official of the Western Han Dynasty. The people loved and supported him as he was generous and kind.

One year, a famine broke out in the regions of the Bohai Sea. More and more bandits surfaced, unsettling the imperial court.

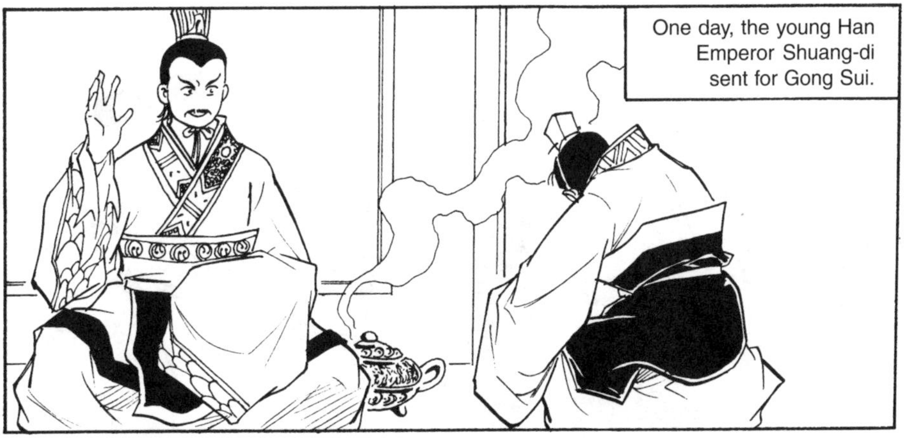

One day, the young Han Emperor Shuang-di sent for Gong Sui.

Gosh, it's sweltering hot! Let's take a break.

All right.

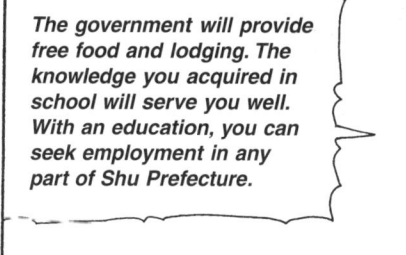

"Yes, it's him. Education has done him a world of good. He's more courteous and civilised now."

Wen Weng was merciful and kind in governing the place. Shu Prefecture became a more civilised society and the people grew richer.

The story of Wen Weng building schools to educate the people is still being told today. For his kind act, Wen Weng was respected through the ages.

Chen Shi Gives Bolts of Cloth to a Thief

During the Eastern Han Dynasty, there was an official by the name of Chen Shi. Being a kind and fair man, Chen Shi was able to judge disputes with impartiality. The people thus loved and supported him greatly.

*The idiomatic phrase "gentleman on the beam" (梁上君子) originated from this story. It refers to a thief or burglar.

Sir, you've made me realise I've done wrong. Please pardon me.

Your repentance shows that you're not entirely wicked. I hope you'll turn over a new leaf.

I'll never steal again, I promise!

I hope I can trust you to keep your word.

Chen Shi then ordered his servant to bring two bolts of cloth.

After selling the cloth, the thief started a small business and earned an honest living.

By showing compassion to the burglar, Chen Shi revealed his kind-hearted nature and showed that a kind act brings dignity and respect to other people.

Physician Dong Feng and the Almond Trees

During the Three Kingdoms Period, there was a physician named Dong Feng who lived at Mt Lu in the State of Wu. He was a skilful physician with a heart of gold.

So many almond trees!

Ohhh ... This pain is unbearable!

Father!

Don't worry, Father. Dong Feng is a good physician and will cure you in no time.

I'll pay him any amount of money he asks for if he can cure me.

No wonder you didn't know Physician Dong doesn't ask his patients to pay. But there's a small request.

Oh? What is it?

Patients who have been cured are asked to plant almond trees in the vicinity.

People with minor illnesses may plant one tree. Those with serious illnesses are to plant five trees.

That explains why the clinic is surrounded by almond trees.

There are more than 100,000 almond trees, all planted by our ex-patients!

My, the almonds sold must have brought in a tidy income.

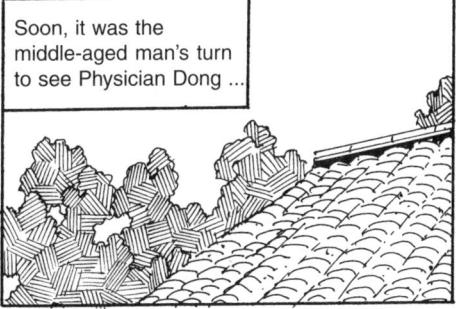

Du Fu Lets Old Lady Pick Dates

Du Fu was a Tang poet who shared equal fame with Li Bai, the great romantic poet in Chinese literature. A man who loved the people and felt their sufferings deeply, Du Fu was a poet with a compassionate heart.

The bright sun livens up the land, Spring breeze sweetened by fragrant flowers and plants. Swallows take wing ...

These date trees seem to have fewer fruits than the rest. Has someone been stealing the dates?

Du Fu suddenly saw an old lady using a stick to pick the dates.

Oh, it's an old lady.

Thank you, sir. You're very kind.

It is nothing.

Soon after, Du Fu moved to another place. A relative by the surname of Wu took over his residence.

Brother Wu, I'm moving to East Village. This house is now yours.

The next day, Du Fu's relative fenced up the yard.

Oh no!

Sir, please be so kind as to let me pick some dates.

Go away!

This is private property. If you want to eat dates, go and buy some!

Sigh. He won't let me pick any dates. What am I going to do?

 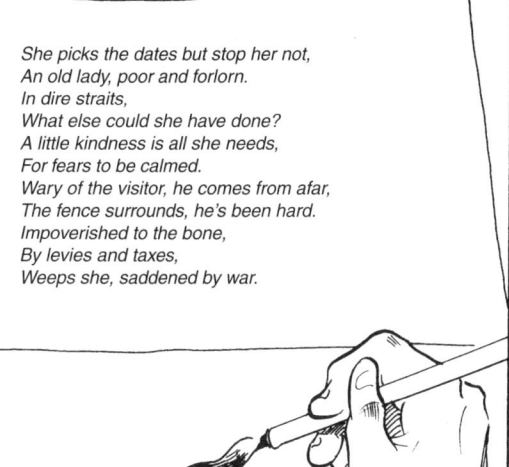

She picks the dates but stop her not,
An old lady, poor and forlorn.
In dire straits,
What else could she have done?
A little kindness is all she needs,
For fears to be calmed.
Wary of the visitor, he comes from afar,
The fence surrounds, he's been hard.
Impoverished to the bone,
By levies and taxes,
Weeps she, saddened by war.

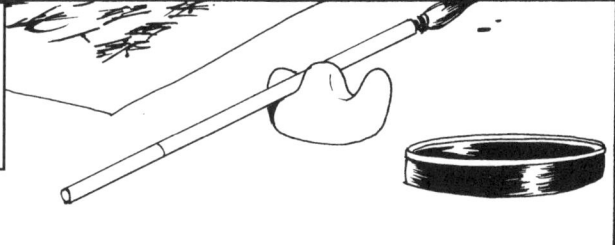

In the poem, which extolled the virtue of kindness, Du Fu censured Master Wu for his callousness and urged him to be sympathetic towards the poor common folk.

Du Fu left before his relative returned. Master Wu was touched by Du Fu's poem.

Brother Du is concerned about the old lady though they are not even distantly related. I've been selfish. I ought to be ashamed of myself.

Master Wu then ordered his servants to remove the fence.

A few days later, Master Wu saw the old lady and stepped forward to help her.

Ma'am, I'm really sorry about what I did. You're welcome to pick the dates any time.

Thank you, sir. You are very kind.

Du Fu's kindness is shown not only in his poems but also by his actions. Everyone who knew him was touched by his kindness.

Fan Zhongyan Puts Concern Before Enjoyment

Fan Zhongyan was a famous politician, militarist and writer who lived during the Northern Song Dynasty. He was a kind man who put the concerns of his country and people before his own.

At 46, Fan Zhongyan was appointed the county magistrate of Suzhou.

Fan Zhongyan's second son, Fan Chunren*

Father ...

Uncle Li said there's a plot of land for sale in Nanyuan. He asked if you'd like to acquire it.

Oh?

*Chunren (纯仁), literally, pure and kind.

"Brother Fan, this house is much too humble for you. It doesn't befit the status of a county magistrate."

Upon hearing those words, Fan Zhongyan merely smiled.

Soon, Fan Zhongyan, his son Chunren and Li Ping came to Nanyuan.

They passed by a beautiful villa ...

Sir, this is a good piece of land. Live here and your family will produce high ministers and great military officers.

Hmm ...

Fengsui Master

Since it is prime land, why don't we build a school here then?

What?!

A school?!

Soon after, Fan Zhongyan bought the plot of land in Nanyuan and built the Suzhou Public School.

At 60, with his own savings, he acquired another 1,000 mu* of farmland for the poor.

*1 mu = 0.0667 hectares

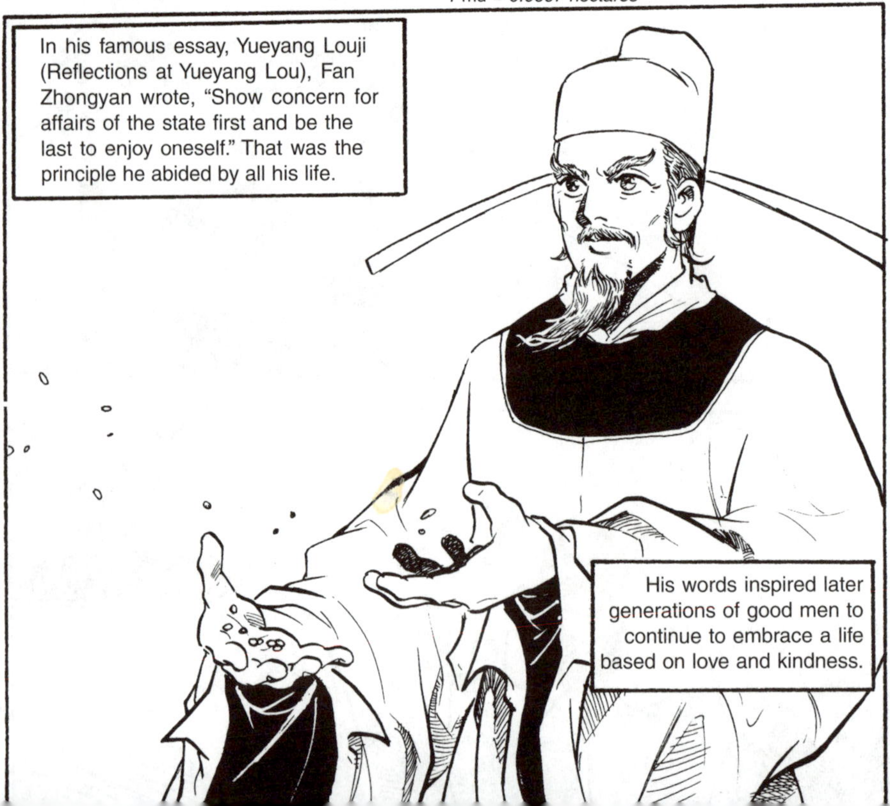

In his famous essay, Yueyang Louji (Reflections at Yueyang Lou), Fan Zhongyan wrote, "Show concern for affairs of the state first and be the last to enjoy oneself." That was the principle he abided by all his life.

His words inspired later generations of good men to continue to embrace a life based on love and kindness.

Su Shi Paints the Fans

Su Shi was a great literary man of the Northern Song Dynasty. He was a talented poet and essayist, outstanding calligrapher and painter. Known for his kindness and righteousness, Su Shi cared for the people and tried his best to solve their problems when he took office as arbitrator in Hangzhou.

Sigh.

It's been raining all summer. No one will think of buying fans in cool weather. How am I going to return the money to Wu Xiao Er?

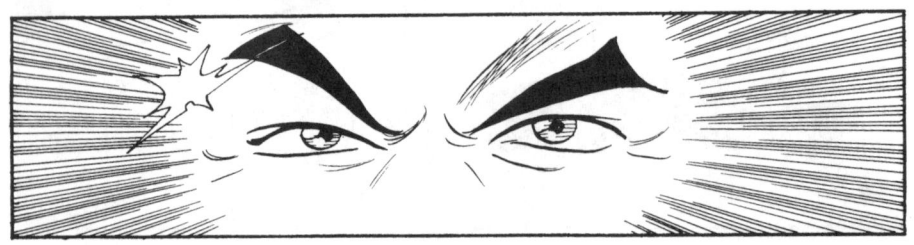

Xu Rang's Happiness Lies in Giving a Helping Hand

During the Ming Dynasty, there was a man by the name of Xu Rang. He was a man of great compassion, admired and praised by all.

One day, when Xu Rang was having his meal ...

Brother, we've come to visit you.

Brother!

Thank you, Uncle, for all your help!

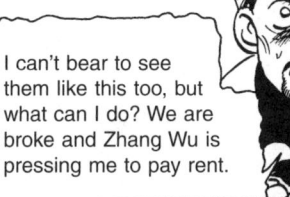

Thank you, Master! Thank you for your kindness!

Oh!

Please get up.

We're fellow villagers. I should help since you're in trouble.

Xu Rang had a kind and compassionate heart. He would extend a helping hand not only to his own relations but also to total strangers.

People thus called him Compassionate Xu Rang and respected him greatly for his humanity and kind-heartedness.

Li Shizhen's
Encyclopedia of Herbs

Li Shizhen, who lived during the Ming Dynasty, was a highly respected and renowned physician and an expert in medicinal herbs.

Four generations of Li Shizhen's family were engaged in medical practice.

Li Shizhen was examining a patient one day when ...

Physician Li, please save my child!

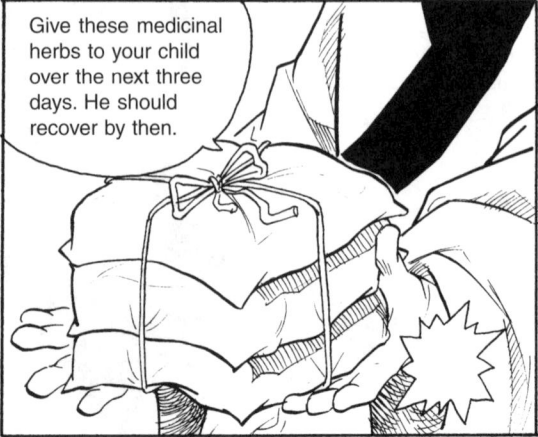

Li Shizhen's mission was motivated by his love for mankind.

He spent his whole life writing the 52-volume *Encyclopedia of Herbs*, which recorded more than 11,000 kinds of herbs.

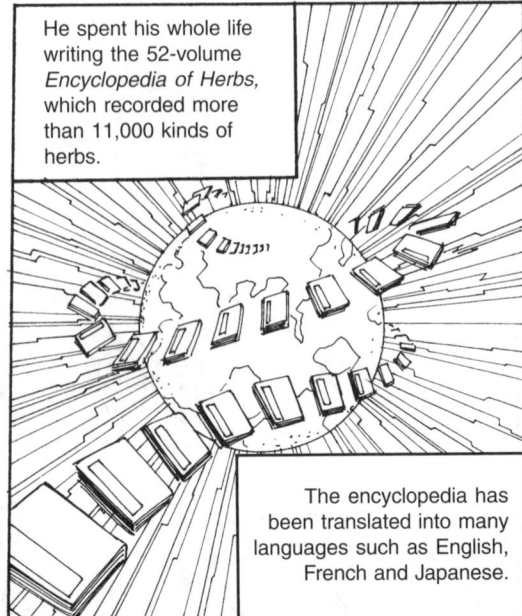

The encyclopedia has been translated into many languages such as English, French and Japanese.

Hailed as the "Greatest Medical Work of the East", the *Encyclopedia of Herbs* has made invaluable contributions to the world of medical science.

ren   kindness; benevolence; love; humanity

Common Terms

仁爱　　[ren ai]　　　kind-heartedness
仁慈　　[ren ci]　　　benevolent; merciful, kind
仁兄　　[ren xiong]　 dear friend
仁义　　[ren yi]　　　kind-heartedness and justice
仁政　　[ren zheng]　 policy of benevolence; benevolent government

Common Expressions

仁民爱物　　　[ren min ai wu]　　　love all the people and animals
仁人君子　　　[ren ren jun zi]　　　a kindly man of noble character
仁人志士　　　[ren ren zhi shi]　　　people with lofty ideals
仁恕之道　　　[ren shu zhi dao]　　way of compassion and benevolence
仁义道德　　　[ren yi dao de]　　　humanity; justice and morality; benevolence
仁义礼智　　　[ren yi li zhi]　　　humanity, justice, propriety and wisdom
仁义之师　　　[ren yi zhi shi]　　　an army of justice
仁者爱人　　　[ren zhe ai ren]　　the benevolent love others
仁者见仁，　　[ren zhe jian ren   the benevolent see benevolence and the wise see
智者见智　　　 zhi zhe jian zhi]   wisdom — different people have different views
仁者乐山，　　[ren zhe le shan   a benevolent man loves the mountains; a wise man
智者乐水　　　 zhi zhe le shui]   loves the sea
仁者无敌　　　[ren zhe wu di]　　the benevolent have no enemy
仁至义尽　　　[ren zhi yi jin]　　　do everything called for by humanity and duty

A Brief Chronology of Chinese History

	夏 Xia Dynasty		About 2100 – 1600 BC
	商 Shang Dynasty		About 1600 – 1100 BC
周 Zhou Dynasty	西周 Western Zhou Dynasty		About 1100 – 771 BC
	東周 Eastern Zhou Dynasty		770 – 256 BC
	春秋 Spring and Autumn Period		770 – 476 BC
	戰國 Warring States		475 – 221 BC
	秦 Qin Dynasty		221 – 207 BC
漢 Han Dynasty	西漢 Western Han		206 BC – AD 24
	東漢 Eastern Han		25 – 220
三國 Three Kingdoms	魏 Wei		220 – 265
	蜀漢 Shu Han		221 – 263
	吳 Wu		222 – 280
	西晉 Western Jin Dynasty		265 – 316
	東晉 Eastern Jin Dynasty		317 – 420
南北朝 Northern and Southern Dynasties	南朝 Southern Dynasties	宋 Song	420 – 479
		齊 Qi	479 – 502
		梁 Liang	502 – 557
		陳 Chen	557 – 589
	北朝 Northern Dynasties	北魏 Northern Wei	386 – 534
		東魏 Eastern Wei	534 – 550
		北齊 Northern Qi	550 – 577
		西魏 Western Wei	535 – 556
		北周 Northern Zhou	557 – 581
	隋 Sui Dynasty		581 – 618
	唐 Tang Dynasty		618 – 907
五代 Five Dynasties	後梁 Later Liang		907 – 923
	後唐 Later Tang		923 – 936
	後晉 Later Jin		936 – 946
	後漢 Later Han		947 – 950
	後周 Later Zhou		951 – 960
宋 Song Dynasty	北宋 Northern Song Dynasty		960 – 1127
	南宋 Southern Song Dynasty		1127 – 1279
	遼 Liao Dynasty		916 – 1125
	金 Jin Dynasty		1115 – 1234
	元 Yuan Dynasty		1271 – 1368
	明 Ming Dynasty		1368 – 1644
	清 Qing Dynasty		1644 – 1911
	中華民國 Republic of China		1912 – 1949
	中華人民共和國 People's Republic of China		1949 –

CHINESE HERITAGE SERIES
Capture the essence of Chinese culture in comics

Enjoy 10% discount and free postage.

Title	Qty	*Price S$	Total
Origins of Chinese Festivals		$14.74	$
Chinese Code of Success: Maxims by Zhu Zi		$14.74	$
Chinese Cuisine		$ 7.50	$
Principles of Feng Shui		$12.51	$
Complete Analects of Confucius Vol 1		$17.61	$
Complete Analects of Confucius Vol 2		$17.61	$
Complete Analects of Confucius Vol 3		$17.61	$

*Prices indicated after 10% discount (GST inclusive)
Offer is for readers in Singapore only.

Send this complete page for your mail order

I wish to purchase the above-mentioned titles at the nett price of S$ _____
Enclosed is my postal order/money order/cheque for S$_____ (No.: _____)
Name (Mr/Mrs/Ms) _____ Tel _____
Address_____
_____ Fax _____
Please charge the amount of S$ _____ to my VISA/MASTER CARD account
(only Visa/Master Card accepted)
Card No. _____ Card Expiry Date _____

Card Holder's Name _____ Signature _____

Send to: **ASIAPAC BOOKS PTE LTD**
　　　　996 Bendemeer Road #06-08/09 Singapore 339944 Tel: (65)3928455 Fax: (65)3926455
Note: Prices quoted valid for purchase by mail order only. Prices subject to change without prior notice.

Values for Success

Subscription Form

Per Issue
Usual: $7.73
Now: $6.80
(local order)

"Values for Success" Comic Series (8 Volumes):
- ☐ Stories of Filial Piety
- ☐ Stories of Loyalty
- ☐ Stories of Integrity
- ☐ Stories of Propriety
- ☐ Stories of Righteousness
- ☐ Stories of Honour
- ☐ Stories of Kindness
- ☐ Stories of Love

I wish to purchase the above-mentioned titles at the nett price of S$ _____
Enclosed is my postal order/money order/cheque for S$_____ (No.: _____)
Name (Mr/Mrs/Ms) _____ Tel _____
Address _____
_____ Fax _____
Please charge the amount of S$ _____ to my VISA/MASTER CARD account
(only Visa/Master Card accepted)
Card No. _____ Card Expiry Date _____

Card Holder's Name _____ Signature _____

Send to: **ASIAPAC BOOKS PTE LTD**
996 Bendemeer Road #06-08/09 Singapore 339944 Tel: (65)3928455 Fax: (65)3926455
Note: Prices quoted valid for purchase by mail order only. Prices subject to change without prior notice.

THE CELESTIAL ZONE
天界无限

Subscription Form

Brand-new martial-art comics by Wee Tian Beng

Per Issue
Usual: S$8.76
Now: S$7.70
(local order)

Published bimonthly. Subscribe now and enjoy fabulous discounts.
I wish to subscribe for *The Celestial Zone* Series
  Singapore Order (free postage):
    ❏ Volumes 1-6 **S$46.20**   ❏ Volumes 1-12 **S$92.40**

  Overseas Order (inclusive of postage by surface mail):
    ❏ Volumes 1-6 **S$61.20**   ❏ Volumes 1-12 **S$122.40**

Enclosed is my postal order/money order/cheque for S$_____ (No.: _____)
Name (Mr/Mrs/Ms) _____ Tel _____
Address _____
_____ Fax _____
Please charge the amount of S$ _____ to my VISA/MASTER CARD account
(only Visa/Master Card accepted)
Card No. _____ Card Expiry Date _____

Card Holder's Name _____ Signature _____

Send to: **ASIAPAC BOOKS PTE LTD**
     996 Bendemeer Road #06-08/09 Singapore 339944 Tel: (65)3928455 Fax: (65)3926455
Note: Prices quoted valid for this mail order only. Prices subject to change without prior notice. Each issue to be mailed to you upon publication — one volume every two months. First issue published in March 1999.

《亚太漫画系列》

成功价值观
仁的故事

编著：陈嘉
绘画：黄庆荣
翻译：吴杰欣

亚太图书有限公司出版